Original title:
Sweet as Pears

Copyright © 2025 Creative Arts Management OÜ
All rights reserved.

Author: Alexander Thornton
ISBN HARDBACK: 978-1-80586-465-3
ISBN PAPERBACK: 978-1-80586-937-5

Savoring the Daylight's End

As daylight fades, with giggles near,
We dance with shadows, holding cheer.
The sun, it winks, with a playful jest,
While twilight joins, it knows no rest.

Laughter bubbles up like soda pop,
With each great sip, we'll never stop.
A silly grin, a joy untamed,
In twilight's glow, we're unashamed.

Melodies of the Ripened Fruit

Oh, the fruit that swings on leafy limbs,
Sometimes it giggles, sometimes it grins.
When juicy laughter drops to the ground,
We catch it quick, it's joy unbound.

A chorus sung by bees and trees,
With rhythmic buzz, we sway in the breeze.
Each bite we take is a funny fate,
A zesty chuckle we cultivate.

The Kiss of Earthly Delights

In gardens where the funny folks grow,
Where every plant puts on a show.
A plump tomato with a cheeky face,
Says, 'Come on over, let's embrace the space!'

With crunchy leaves that tickle and tease,
And carrots that wiggle with graceful ease.
We feast with laughter, indulge with glee,
In this banquet of joy, we're all so free.

Whispers of the Rustic Charm

Amid the fields, where giggles bloom,
The rustic charm dispels the gloom.
With playful breezes that tickle our toes,
Nature whispers secrets that nobody knows.

We chase the clouds, play tag with the sun,
In this whimsical world, we all are one.
As evening falls, our laughter's a song,
In the dance of dusk, we all belong.

Juices of Joy

In a fruit bowl high, giggles swirl,
A plump little fruit begins to twirl.
With every bite, a burst of cheer,
Laughter dances, bringing us near.

Friends gather round, their eyes aglow,
Trading jests in that fruit-filled show.
Munching and crunching, a joyful spree,
Each slice sprinkles mirth, oh, glee!

Orchard Whispers

In the orchard's hush, a chuckle brews,
Ripe laughter ripens in each morning dew.
The branches sway with playful might,
As fruit takes flight, what a silly sight!

Beneath the leaves, secrets exchange,
A pear winks slyly, as if to arrange.
With blissful grins and playful cheer,
Nature's jesters, we hold dear!

Nectar in the Breeze

A breeze blows in with a tickling tease,
Making pears giggle on their leafy knees.
Sticky fingers and bright, shiny grins,
Who knew fruit could spark such silly spins?

Buzzing bees join the merry parade,
Sipping nectar, they're laughter made.
With every drop, joy flies and sways,
Life's simple pleasures are funnier ways!

Golden Fruit Dreams

Golden orbs resting under the sun,
Jokes unfold, oh, this is pure fun!
Dancing in sunlight, they laugh with ease,
Whispers of joy rustle through the leaves.

From twilight till dawn, the banter flows,
With every bite, a new punchline grows.
As we munch and chuckle, life seems right,
These golden dreams bring pure delight!

The Heartbeat of the Harvest

In orchards where the laughter grows,
With fruits that dance in shiny rows,
The apples giggle, and grapes play tag,
As squirrels high-five in a joyful brag.

The pumpkins roll like bowling balls,
With hidden tricks in their plump halls,
A carrot wears a snazzy hat,
While rhubarb juggles on the mat.

Liquid Sunshine Dripping Gold

In jars that twinkle like stars at night,
The nectar flows, a golden sight,
Bottles cheer like little friends,
As toast toasts and laughter blends.

A drizzle here, a squirt up there,
Like sunshine caught in cozy air,
Pancakes bounce like they're on the rise,
With syrup dreams and syrupy sighs.

A Playground of Color and Flavor

In gardens bright with comic flair,
Tomatoes giggle in the summer air,
Carrots leap in leaps of joy,
While little peas play hide and ploy.

Radishes bounce on their leafy feet,
Mixing colors in a fun treat,
Spinach flexes, gets all pumped,
As broccoli gets whimsically chumped.

Embracing the Touch of Earth

In muddy boots and happy toil,
We dig up gems from fertile soil,
With worms that joke and critters that dance,
Nature's party, let's take a chance!

The daisies twirl, the bees serenade,
While we splash in the blissful glade,
As fruits and veggies form a crew,
Throwing laughter like a rain of dew.

Pure Bliss in Vines' Embrace

In the garden, laughter grows,
With squishy fruit and nose-wrinkled prose.
Bouncing round like summersweets,
Who knew fruits had such funny feats?

Swinging branches, full of cheer,
Tree-hugging squirrels, oh dear!
Wobbling vines in sunshine's glare,
Nature's comedy, beyond compare!

The Dance of Ripening Days

Days drift by on giggly rays,
Fruitful frolic in silly ways.
Swaying gently, like a mood,
Grapes whisper tales of pure food!

A wobbly peach takes a spin,
The apricot grins, joins in.
With every bounce, a chuckle shines,
The fruit parade of funny vines!

Refreshing Embraces of Nature

Nature's joke, a fruity play,
A juice splash brightens the day.
Sticky fingers, giggles spread,
Look out! The berry's hit your head!

Chasing ducks by the pond's edge,
Fragrant fruits promise a pledge.
To keep the laughter ever near,
Beneath the branches, all is clear!

A Mosaic of Digested Dreams

Dreams blend in a fruity swirl,
With every bite, the world may twirl.
Pineapple jokes out on a limb,
Lemon's laugh, a splashy whim!

Oranges giggle in the sun,
In their zest, they have such fun.
A tapestry of silly scenes,
Nature's canvas, full of beans!

Lush Green Bliss

In a garden full of giggles,
With fruits that dance and sway,
The leaves play tag with sunshine,
While birds hum tunes, hooray!

Round and round, the children run,
Chasing shadows soft and light,
While juicy gems hang from branches,
Making every day feel bright.

Cradled in Softness

Fluffier than a pillow fight,
These fruits roll round with glee,
Bouncing off a playful breeze,
As bright as they can be.

Underneath the bubble trees,
We laugh till we can't stand,
Each juicy prize smiles back at us,
In this fruity wonderland.

Orchard's Warm Embrace

The trees wear hats of leafy green,
While roots tickle through the ground,
In this place of fruity fun,
Joy and laughter can be found.

Sunbeams hug the ripening crew,
As giggles fill the air,
With every plump and happy bite,
We hold our happiness with flair.

Ripened Radiance

Each round delight in colors bright,
Winks at me with a grin,
They've found a way to laugh and play,
In this harvest, we all win.

Sipping smiles from the orchard,
With silly faces all around,
The fruits invite their merry pals,
To dance upon the ground.

Ripe Aromas of Togetherness

In a garden wide and bright,
Laughter blooms, a pure delight.
With chubby cheeks and joyful cheers,
We dance beneath the golden spheres.

Fond memories in every bite,
Juices dripping, such a sight!
We twirl like fruits in sunny rays,
Creating joy in silly ways.

Sun-Kissed Segments of Life

Round and plump, we giggle loud,
Underneath the leafy shroud.
Chasing critters, running fast,
Catching rays that always last.

With each slice, a silly face,
Sticky fingers, a wild race!
As we munch and laugh and play,
Sun-kissed fun is here to stay.

Honeyed Moments in the Grove

In the grove where laughter rings,
Sticky paws and feathery wings.
We share our fruit and share our dreams,
Amid the laughter, joy redeems.

Fuzzy hats and goofy grins,
Always giggling, who really wins?
With every morsel that we share,
We find a giggle everywhere.

The Tapestry of Golden Seasons

Seasons flip like pages turn,
Golden hues in bright discern.
With every bite, a chuckle flows,
Life's rich harvest, oh, how it grows!

Jumping petals, chasing leaves,
Woven tales of silly weaves.
In this tapestry we roam,
With each laugh, we feel at home.

Whimsical Journeys of the Soul

In a land where socks all dance and twirl,
Giddy hats chase dreams, in a vibrant whirl.
Bouncing on bubbles, they float to the ground,
Chasing laughter, joy is always found.

Kites flap their wings, wearing goofy grins,
While spoons and forks trade gossip about sins.
With a wink, the clouds play hide and seek,
Amidst giggles, the sun blinks cheekily.

The jellybeans hop, in colors so bright,
Swinging on swings, they take flight at night.
Chuckle with cherries, they dance on the breeze,
Tickling the nose of the buzzing honeybees.

Every wink of the stars is a chance to glow,
For the silly souls, in this fun little show.
Join in the revels, let your spirit soar,
In giggling echoes, there's always more!

The Aroma of Togetherness

Whipped cream and drizzle, oh what a dream,
With sprinkles that giggle and dance in a stream.
Fruit salad shadows create such a fuss,
As bananas wear hats, joining the buzz.

Lemonade laughter spills on the lawn,
While cookies debate who will sing the dawn.
In puddles of jelly, the rainbows collide,
As friends find their voices in joy, side by side.

Each spoonful of joy, a memory made,
With laughter that bounces, never will fade.
Toasting with muffins as time starts to fly,
In the aroma of love, we cheer and comply.

The aroma of glee fills the sunlit air,
While nutty encounters lead us to care.
So, gather round closely, let's savor the fun,
In this festival of joy, we're all number one!

Laughter Swirling in the Harvest Air

Corn on the cob sings with merry delight,
While pumpkins wear hats, all ready for night.
The apples are giggling, dressed in their best,
As scarecrows compete in a quirky jest.

Bouncing on hay bales, the squirrels join in,
Twirling their tails like a dance to begin.
Cider soars high in a sneaky balloon,
Carved faces chuckle under the harvest moon.

With every soft rustle, the giggles appear,
In the middle of bounty, there's nothing to fear.
So raise up your voices in playful cheer,
For laughter and joy are what we hold dear.

In the swirling breeze, let the jokes take flight,
As we relish the magic spun on this night.
With glee in our hearts, we'll dance as we sway,
In the harvest of laughter, come join us and play!

The Warmth of the Orchard's Heart

In the orchard where the laughter flows,
Fruits wear smiles, and the sunshine glows.
Beneath the boughs, the squirrels dance,
While bees hum tunes, given half a chance.

Jokes are ripe on the branches high,
With wobbly pears, oh my, oh my!
They giggle away with a gentle sway,
Saying, "Come munch and laugh all day!"

A Canvas of Heavenly Flavors

Colors splash like a painter's dream,
Fruitful silhouettes in the sunlight beam.
Pears wear hats; it's a fashion show,
Strutting their stuff in a breezy flow.

Lemonade's jealous, a bitter old gal,
While sauce and jam try to throw a pal.
But in this orchard, joy reigns supreme,
With fruit so funny, it's silly but gleam!

Peace Gathered on the Branches

Under blossoms, the breezes tease,
Fruit hangouts filled with worms and cheese.
Chasing dreams on a fluffy cloud,
Pears and pals laugh, all happy and loud.

Each branch a throne, a leafy retreat,
Where fruity conversations are light and sweet.
Ripe with glee, they share a jest,
In this orchard, yarns never rest.

Flavorful Fantasies of the Season

A circus of flavor in the summer sun,
With juggling fruits, oh what fun!
A pear with glasses reads the news,
While grapes in tuxedos share their views.

Tickle your taste buds with a giggle or two,
As juicy tales spill, bright and true.
In this patch of fun and fruity cheers,
We toast to flavors, forget all fears!

A Tapestry of Nature's Comfort

In the orchard where fruit flutters,
There's laughter that tickles and mutters.
The trees wear coats of green and gold,
Tickling the toes of the young and old.

A squirrel with a nutty grin,
Has a dance that makes the world spin.
While bees buzz by, wearing shades,
Creating sweet chaos, nature's charades.

The wind whispers secrets of joy,
As happy birds play with a toy.
With grass stains on their knees, they cheer,
In a land where worry can't appear.

Frogs in the pond croak out a tune,
While crickets serenade the full moon.
Here laughter is ripe, like the fruit on the tree,
A tapestry of mirth, wild and free.

Dew-kissed Secrets of Bliss

Morning dew dances on leaves so bright,
While bugs hold a rave under soft moonlight.
Oh, the chipmunk's a DJ, don't you know?
Switching tracks like a pro at a show.

With a splash in the puddles, kids leap high,
Chasing rainbows that emerge from the sky.
Nature giggles as thunderous rolls,
Imagining concerts for warm-hearted souls.

Petals whisper jokes that make you grin,
As old trees nod with a crinkly chin.
The melody of laughter fills the air,
Dew-kissed secrets without a care.

Fireflies flicker, putting on a bash,
The best party happens in nature's splash.
And when day ends, stars twinkle, you see,
The best moments are ripe, happy, and free.

Nature's Vibrant Serenade

What a show, the flowers are singing,
With colors that dance and are swinging.
Bees wear tuxedos, ready to buzz,
Throwing a party just because!

In the meadow, a cow takes the stage,
Doing the cha-cha, it's all the rage.
With a hoof and a horn, they tango with glee,
Mooing along in a jamboree.

The wind blows softly, a gentle tease,
Calling all critters, come shake your knees!
The trees sway to their favorite tune,
Underneath the watchful eye of the moon.

Nature chuckles in vibrant delight,
In every corner, laughter takes flight.
With each giggle a blossom appears,
A serenade full of joy, never fears.

Harmony of Softness and Light

Beneath the sun, the flowers squeak,
As bunnies hop and play hide and seek.
With petals that shimmer, each laugh is bright,
In this gentle chaos, all feels just right.

The clouds puff up, like cotton candy,
Birds on a swing, oh isn't it dandy?
Every leaf whispers a ticklish tale,
As nature winks and lets laughter sail.

Pigs roll over in warm, soft mud,
Painting the fields in a gooey flood.
Joy is a splash, and the puddles grow,
In the sweetest fun, let the giggles flow.

Under the trees where the sun filters down,
Life's a parade, no hint of a frown.
In this harmony of ease and delight,
Nature is simply a pure, funny sight.

Sweet Indulgence Wrapped in Leaves

In the orchard's embrace, they play,
Juicy morsels bright as the day.
With laughter, we munch, oh what a feat,
Fruity giggles, our favorite treat.

Their blushy skin, a whimsical sight,
A dance of delight in the warm sunlight.
We devour with glee, feeling quite grand,
Nature's candy tucked in our hands.

Radiant Threads of Afternoon

Beneath the tree's sprawling shade,
A parade of snacks, perfectly laid.
With each juicy bite, our troubles break,
Laughter erupts with each tasty take.

The golden glow in this playful scene,
Smiles abound as we munch on the green.
Our sticky fingers tell tales of fun,
In this fruity frolic, we're never done.

The Lullaby of the Orchard Breeze

Whispers in leaves, a gentle tease,
As we giggle and snack with the breeze.
Portions of joy, rolled into each bite,
A comical dance under sunlight bright.

The squirrels join in, oh, what a show!
Dancing around as we put on the show.
Our laughter mingles with the rustling trees,
In this orchard of fun, our hearts find ease.

A Carnival of Flavorful Moments

Step right up to this fruity affair,
Gleeful munchers, without a care.
Each juicy orb a ticket to cheer,
With every bite, the joy draws near.

Round and round, we spin and sway,
A delicious ride on this fun-filled day.
With smiles wide, we taste and play,
In our carnival of laughter, come what may.

Nature's Sugared Melody

In the orchard where we frolic,
Laughter bounces off the trees.
Fruits giggle, skins so frolic,
Dancing in the warm, soft breeze.

Leaves whisper silly tales around,
Bouncing humor in the sun.
Plump and jolly, laughter's sound,
Nature's joke is just begun.

The branches sway, a merry jig,
Squirrels mimic every cheer.
Branches stretch, they jump and dig,
Tickling fruits from far and near.

With each bite, we burst with giggles,
Juicy jokes drip down our chin.
As cotton candy, nature wiggles,
A fruity feast ensures we grin.

Embracing the Season

As summer's warmth begins to linger,
Frogs wear crowns, the birds all sing.
Nature's laughter, a playful finger,
To all the joys the season brings.

Picnics set with fruits galore,
Ants parade a march of fun.
Silly hats the squirrels wore,
A feast for everyone—except the bun!

Melons flop like clumsy clowns,
With juice that splashes, oooh and ahh!
Sunshine waves from golden crowns,
Tickling toes of all who saw.

Embrace the giggles in the breeze,
Nature's voice, a hearty cheer.
Every moment's sure to please,
Full of humor, joys appear.

Pear Perfume in the Air

In the orchard, scents arise,
Perfumed laughter fills the sky.
Fragrant jokes in sweet disguise,
Whirling whispers, oh my, oh my!

The golden globes hang in a row,
Offering giggles, one by one.
Each bite bursts with a jokester's glow,
The fruit parade has just begun.

Bouncing bees wear tiny hats,
Buzzing jokes, they twirl and glide.
With every step, the humor chats,
As fragrance bursts, we laugh with pride.

Ticklish vines sway to the song,
As melodies of fruit combine.
We join the chorus, loud and strong,
In nature's laughter, we align.

Taste of Gentle Indulgence

A feast of flavors, rich delight,
Fruits share stories, funny, bright.
Sugar-glossed with every bite,
Savoring smiles under soft light.

With each nibble, giggles soar,
Tummies twist in playful ways.
As if the fruits were made for more,
Indulgence fills our sunlit days.

Friends all gather, spoons in hand,
Building castles of delight.
Life's a banquet, so well planned,
Where every moment feels just right.

So let's indulge, share some cheer,
With every taste, let laughter rise.
In this feast, we have no fear,
Every fruit a sweet surprise!

Bottled Sunshine in Each Bite

Juicy bursts of golden cheer,
Laughter dances, draws us near.
Bottled sunshine in a crack,
Taking giggles, never slack.

Fuzzy skins and squishy dreams,
Silly faces, silly screams.
Take a bite, a giggle flows,
Wobbly bites, a friend it shows.

Jars of joy upon the shelf,
Eating laughter, better than wealth.
Fruit-filled capers, oh what fun,
Making memories, one by one.

Tangy Tales of Togetherness

Once there was a fruit so rare,
Bringing smiles with fruity flair.
Tangy bites and giggles shared,
In every moment, love declared.

Let's squeeze the juice of joyful days,
Where laughter leads in playful ways.
Join the feast, the fruits align,
With each chuckle, we intertwine.

Fruity chaos, sticky hands,
Petty fights and food demands.
Friendship sealed with every slice,
Whimsical bites, oh how nice!

Chasing the Last Light of Day

As daylight fades to shades of gold,
Giggles rise, silly stories told.
Under the sun's warm, glowing gaze,
Chasing shadows that twist and graze.

Frisky friends in a fruit-filled race,
Lemony laughter lights up the place.
Every bite, a cheer ring,
Each new joke, our spirits sing.

Pearly juices, the night does call,
With every bite, we'll never fall.
Under skies of twilight hue,
Joyful hearts, just me and you.

Blossoms in the Twilight Air

Blossoms whisper in the breeze,
Ticklish greens and gentle tease.
Fruity laughter fills the night,
Petals swaying, a silly sight.

Chasing shadows, swinging wide,
Sweet floral scents, we run and glide.
In the twilight, we unite,
Fleeting moments, pure delight.

With each munch, the taste does twirl,
In our syrupy, silly world.
Let's hold hands and laugh out loud,
With fruity dreams, we're strong and proud.

Nectar of the Gentle Breeze

In the orchard where giggles sway,
The fruit does a dance and play,
With every bite, a chuckle grows,
As juicy tales begin to flow.

Bees buzz with a comical hum,
While squirrels search for snacks to come,
Each pear a jester in disguise,
Tickling taste buds, oh what a surprise!

Friends gather 'neath the shady tree,
Sharing laughter with glee and glee,
The breeze carries whispers bright,
Of fruity jokes that take flight.

So let us savor this sunny tease,
For joy is ripe upon the breeze,
In every bite, a playful cheer,
Orchard pranks we hold so dear.

Harvested Hues of Joy

In fields where colors blend and play,
The harvest sends us on our way,
With cheeky smiles and silly grins,
We gather round to share our wins.

A patchwork quilt of fruity cheer,
Beneath the sun, we feast and cheer,
Each pear a gem, a giggling muse,
Creating chaos we can't refuse.

Oh, how they tumble, how they roll,
Peculiar antics take control,
In every slice, a laugh awaits,
For jokes are shared on fruit-filled plates.

A harvest bold, a joyful spree,
With every bite, pure ecstasy,
As laughter bounces on the breeze,
In hues of joy, we find our ease.

Luscious Loaves of Remembrance

A baker's dream, fresh from the hearth,
With loaves that giggle, oh what mirth,
A sprinkle of laughter in every crumb,
   As fruity flavors beat the drum.

Yeast on the rise, their spirits soar,
Baking mayhem ignites the floor,
Each loaf a riddle, a raucous tale,
   Of fruity laughter without fail.

Friends gather round to taste, to share,
With perky smiles and wild hair,
The scent of joy wafts through the air,
As lunchtime turns to lighthearted dare.

In every slice, a memory blooms,
Of laughter lost in doughy rooms,
We savor moments as they pass,
In luscious loaves, we raise our glass.

Orchard's Embrace

Under the canopy, we find our fun,
In an orchard tickled by the sun,
Where pears hang low with playful glee,
Chasing our worries, wild and free.

Pigs in the shade, they snort and roll,
While we munch on fruit and lose control,
Every hearty laugh, a juicy prize,
As we dance beneath the pear tree skies.

The branches sway, the laughter rings,
As we celebrate the joy that springs,
From every bite and every jest,
In orchard's arms, we are all blessed.

So come, my friends, let's raise a cheer,
For silly moments we hold dear,
In every pear, a story waits,
As laughter echoes through the gates.

The Language of Sunlight and Soil

In the garden, giggles bloom,
Where vines weave tales of sunny gloom.
The soil whispers, 'Dance and sway,'
As earthworms chuckle at the play.

Bees buzz jokes in the bright air,
While butterflies flaunt without a care.
The tomatoes, red with glee,
Challenge cucumbers, "Race with me!"

Mice in tiny capes take flight,
Squeaky laughter fills the night.
Sunlight paints the leaves so green,
In this veggie world, the fun's unseen.

With every sprout and leafy twist,
Who knew that dirt could bring such bliss?
Listen close, you'll hear the jest,
In sunlight and soil, we are truly blessed.

Velvet Touch on Tender Skin

The summer breeze, a soft embrace,
Tickles cheeks, a playful chase.
The flowers blush, they can't resist,
As sunbeams dance in a golden mist.

Leaves rustle secrets, sweet and sly,
While raindrops giggle as they pass by.
Tickle me pink, says the rose so fine,
A fungi's laugh, in the sun, they dine.

Sunlight winks, a cheeky muse,
Underneath skies of vibrant hues.
A little plant with leafy ears,
Hums a tune to coax out cheers.

In every petal, joy bestowed,
Nature's whims, a light-hearted ode.
With every touch, a chuckle kind,
The velvet grass, our laughter blind.

A Basket Full of Love

A basket brims with fruity delight,
Oranges giggle, just out of sight.
Strawberries wink, all dressed in red,
As avocados joke about their spread.

Plums roll down, a lively spree,
Peaches say, "Come play with me!"
Melons giggle, oh what a sight,
Under the sun, their hearts feel light.

Lemon's zest, sharp and bright,
Jests of tang, a playful bite.
In this grove, there's no goodbyes,
Each fruit a laugh beneath the skies.

Filled to the brim, this basket bright,
Shines with joy, it feels just right.
Gather 'round, let's share the cheer,
For laughter's best when friends are near.

Nature's Gentle Caress

The daisies dance with playful glee,
As breezes tickle, wild and free.
Crickets chirp in carefree song,
In nature's arms, we all belong.

Clouds puff up, parade in style,
Rain drops giggle, 'Stay a while.'
Sunlight glistens on gentle streams,
Nature hums with joyous dreams.

Butterflies flutter, a comic show,
Wings of colors in ebb and flow.
Hummingbirds sip, tea party for two,
A botanical bash, just me and you.

In every rustle, find the jest,
Life's a garden, we're all guests.
With every breeze, a gentle tease,
Nature's laughter brings such ease.

Bliss Wrapped in Nature's Arms

In the orchard, we all dance,
With the fruits that make us prance.
Laughter echoes through the trees,
As we munch on juicy tease.

A squirrel steals a tasty bite,
While we giggle in delight.
Nature's bounty, oh so grand,
Brings us joy, and sticky hands.

Beneath the sun, we lie and play,
Counting clouds that float away.
The taste of laughter fills the air,
As we share without a care.

With every fruity, fizzy drink,
We toast to joy, and not to think.
Life's a feast, let's cheer and shout,
In the orchard, there's no doubt.

Flavors of a Nostalgic Feast

Remember when we plucked all day,
Chasing giggles in a fray?
With faces smeared in shades of gold,
Our antics never growing old.

Cider bubbles in our cups,
As we jump and spill it up.
The backyard blooms in wild excess,
A joyful, fruity, funny mess.

Old recipes, they dance and swirl,
As we ponder what to twirl.
Each dish is like a silly game,
With friendly banter just the same.

Grandma's pies take center stage,
While Uncle Fred talks in a rage.
Flavors mix with laughter's tune,
Beneath the watchful golden moon.

Threads of Golden Memories

A picnic blanket, spread so wide,
With fruity snacks we cannot hide.
The breeze whispers funny tales,
Of flying pies and pear-shaped whales.

We spun around, in circles fast,
Until our little legs all passed.
Giggles echoed through the glade,
As fruit baskets started to fade.

Sticky fingers and cheeky grins,
Letting all the silly begin.
With every crunch, we laugh aloud,
Silly stories shared with crowd.

As shadows grow and night descends,
We share the fun with all our friends.
Those golden moments, oh so bright,
Are woven deep into the night.

The Essence of Orchard Secrets

Whispers of the fruit trees call,
As we play hopscotch—head over heels.
The secrets that the orchard keeps,
Are found in laughter, dives, and leaps.

A banana peel, a slippery breeze,
A game of dodge with silly trees.
We giggle as we trip and fall,
Nature's game becomes our all.

The taste of wonder fills our grin,
As we chase after the wind's spin.
Orchard's heart beats wild and free,
With just enough of silly glee.

So grab a pear and join the fun,
A sticky mess for everyone.
In these moments, joy is found,
In every taste, let's twirl around.

The Taste of Summer Days

Under the sun, we dance all day,
Giggles echo, as children play.
Juicy bites of laughter burst,
In every sunny, giggly burst.

Lemonade spills, bright yellow cheer,
While ants prepare a feast, oh dear!
Chasing each other, we tumble and roll,
Life's a flavor, oh how we stroll!

With sticky fingers and hungry grins,
We munch on joy, as the fun begins.
The taste of summer, wild and free,
Is a tongue-twisting recipe!

So grab a slice of fun today,
And let your worries drift away.
For in this moment, laughter sways,
Life's a picnic, in many ways!

Sugary Cascade

On a riverbank where giggles flow,
Chocolate fountains steal the show.
With each dip, a splash of mirth,
As laughter fills the sugary birth.

Meringue floats like fluffy dreams,
Cotton candy bursts at the seams.
Pies are flying, what a scene,
A right hilarious sugar machine!

Lollipops spin in a whirl of fun,
Chasing rainbows, we dash and run.
The air is thick with sweet delight,
A tummy tickle, purest flight!

So dip your toes in this delight,
And let your cares take flight tonight.
In this cascade of joyful glee,
Grab a treat, come laugh with me!

Harvest Moon Serenade

Under the harvest moon's soft glow,
We gather laughter, let it flow.
With baskets full of giggles tight,
We dance and play throughout the night.

Pumpkins roll, a funny sight,
As shadows play, the moon is bright.
Apple bobbing, who will win?
With silly splashes, the fun begins!

Cider flows, a joyous cheer,
While squirrel friends join us near.
We toast to joy with cups held high,
Underneath this twinkling sky!

So let us share this moonlit song,
With belly laughs that last so long.
In every drop, a memory stored,
In harvest's dance, we're never bored!

Fragrant Delights

In the garden, scents collide,
With bouquets bursting, we take a ride.
Rosemary tickles, basil sighs,
Zesty aromas spark giggly highs.

Muffins rise, a sweet surprise,
With every bite, a cheeky prize.
Herbs and spices do their dance,
In this fragrant, frolicsome romance!

Jam on toast, sticky smiles spread,
As we share stories, filling our heads.
Rhubarb whispers as muffins puff,
Among the spices, life is fun stuff!

So join the feast, let laughter bloom,
Share your flavor in this room.
For in each dish, we find delight,
A playful heart, a recipe bright!

Bright Bites of Happiness

In the orchard, laughter grows,
With giggles flying like butterflies.
Tasting sunshine wrapped in leaves,
The fruit is winking, oh what a surprise!

Juicy whispers, juicy dreams,
Sipping nectar, oh what a scene.
Chasing raindrops, laughing loud,
In a world where freedom's keen.

Plump little treasures on my plate,
Dancing colors, oh how they gleam.
Biting into blissful fate,
Every crunch, a happy scream!

Under stars with sticky hands,
No shame in this fruity delight.
We feast like kings in wondrous lands,
While giggles echo through the night.

Nature's Gentle Caress

A tender pat from nature's hand,
Beneath the trees where we all play.
Tickling toes in soft green grass,
While teasing shadows seem to sway.

The breeze is laughing, oh so sly,
Freckled sunlight dancing by.
Each little fruit a cheeky grin,
With nature's charm, we cannot lie.

Banana peels, a slippery joke,
As laughter spills from trees so high.
We stumble, giggle, smile and choke,
On nature's quirks, oh my, oh my!

In the garden, joy does sprout,
As bees buzz tunes in sweet refrain.
A ticklish hug from every route,
With every sigh, we dance again.

Luscious Layers of Life

In every layer, joy unfolds,
A slice of laughter, crisp and bright.
The fruity layers tease and tickle,
Each bite's a daydream, pure delight.

Yummy stories packed like pies,
Each flavor tells a silly tale.
So many giggles in disguise,
In every bite, a happy trail.

Fruits in harmony swirl around,
The orchard's symphony takes flight.
Jokes are hidden in the ground,
Where roots chuckle in pure delight.

With every layer, life expands,
A slice of joy, a splat of cheer.
In every fruit, the laughter stands,
Let's eat it up, year after year!

The Abundance of Lushness

The garden spills with colors bright,
As veggies wiggle, dance, and sway.
Tomatoes blush with pure delight,
While pumpkins grin and sway in play.

Berries giggle, baskets cheer,
Fruits of laughter everywhere.
With buttercups that prance and twirl,
A feast that brings us all to share.

With every nibble, laughter blooms,
As nature's taste buds tickle us.
A banquet grand of silly tunes,
Come join the feast! Not fuss, just fuss!

Underneath the sunny glow,
We dance and twirl without a care.
With nature's gifts, we steal the show,
In luscious lushness, joy to wear!

Daydreams in the Fruitful Shadows

Beneath the leaves, I find my seat,
A chubby squirrel, a fruit to greet.
He winks at me, a nutty grin,
I swear he thinks he'll always win.

A bumblebee buzzes, full of cheer,
It lands on me and whispers, 'Dear,
You look delicious, come dance around!'
I laugh and spin without a sound.

The sunbeam tickles, the hammock sways,
While ants parade in silly displays.
They march like soldiers, but oh so slow,
Their picnic plans, a grand tableau.

And here I think, life's like a pie,
Some slices sweet, and some awry.
With juicy flavors that mold the day,
I'll dance and laugh the hours away.

Nature's Palette of Delicacies

The orchard blooms with colors bright,
A rainbow feast, what sheer delight!
A frog in green with a hat of leaves,
Sings me tales that the wind weaves.

A parrot squawks, 'You're looking fine!'
I shout back, 'And you, divine!'
We swap our secrets, crafty and bold,
In this wild garden, legends unfold.

Ripe peaches tumble, oh what a sight,
They roll and giggle with pure delight.
They trick the bees with their juicy flair,
Requesting free hugs, a fruity affair!

A melon laughs, 'Don't take it hard,
Life's a joke, we're all a card!'
With each laugh shared, I feel so free,
In nature's art, we're harmony.

Reflections in a Sunlit Glade

In the glade where shadows play,
A chipmunk juggles, what a display!
His acorns roll, a clumsy show,
I can't help chuckling, 'Go, little bro!'

The daisies whisper, 'Join the fun!'
As I toss pies, they slip and run.
A pudding fight bursts in full bloom,
Splattering joy, banishing gloom.

The breeze brings laughter from afar,
With singing sparrows, the morning star.
They serenade me, their notes so spry,
In this sun-drenched place, I can't deny.

As twilight paints with hues of grace,
I wave goodbye to this silly space.
And ponder how life's a delightful jest,
Where joy's the fruit, and laughter's the best.

Echoes of Childhood in the Grove

In the grove where dreams take flight,
A kid once slipped, what a funny sight!
With a splat and a giggle, mud flies high,
His friends erupt with laughter to the sky.

Old trees chuckle, sharing tales,
Of grapevine swings and paper sails.
They recall the games, the secret trails,
The clumsy tumbles, and fishy gales.

A cat naps on a picnic spread,
While crumbs of cookies dance in his head.
The sunbeams twinkle from leaf to leaf,
As giggles arise, infectious and brief.

So here we sit, in this lovely place,
With memories wrapped in a warm embrace.
Childhood echoes, sweet memories thrive,
In the grove of laughter, we feel alive.

Laughter Echoes Under the Canopy

In the orchard where giggles bloom,
The fruit hangs low, a jolly room.
Bees buzz tunes as they flirt and whirl,
Chasing the breeze, watch the leaves twirl.

A squirrel cracks jokes with a pear in tow,
While the shadowy branches sway to and fro.
Two kids chase dreams on their toes so fleet,
Tripping on laughter, a delightful treat.

The sun plays tag, casting playful light,
Tickling the branches, oh what delight!
Nature's own stand-up, a merry show,
Each giggle ripples, a joyous flow.

In this fruity circus, folks gather round,
For smiles and chuckles in abundance found.
So raise your glass for the mirth we share,
In the fruit-filled haven, life's beyond compare.

Radiance Dripping from Branches

Juicy gems hang with a cheeky grin,
While the tree winks in the sun's warm spin.
Laughter drips like dew from the leaves,
Tickling our toes like playful thieves.

A pair of birds argue, then start to sing,
As if debating who's queen of the fling!
Wobbling branches, their performance grand,
Droplets of joy fall like glittering sand.

Each pear a joke, bursting bright and bold,
With stories of summers and secrets untold.
The clouds, they chuckle, as shadows are cast,
With the knack to make our sweet moments last.

Children prance, with mischief in their eyes,
Imagining worlds where the fruitiest flies.
In this giggle-filled garden, hearts take flight,
Radiance spills over, oh what a sight!

The Color of Heartfelt Joy

In shades of green, the laughter grows,
Each pear a secret, nobody knows.
Grinning faces filter through the trees,
Giggling whispers dance in the breeze.

A dog wearing sunglasses thinks he's the best,
While robins in bow ties prepare for a jest.
With splashes of humor and shimmers of play,
This orchard's a stage where we laugh all day.

The splendor of smiles, colors collide,
With happiness dripping like bright summer tide.
Playful shadows twist, twirl, and pop,
In this joyous realm, there's never a stop.

As twilight approaches, the stars come alive,
Encouraging chuckles while crickets connive.
With hearts wide open, we dance in delight,
Beneath the pear tree, emotions take flight.

Delectable Sunlight Dances

Bouncing beams of joy flicker and twirl,
As the orchard joins in a whimsical whirl.
Each pear pelts down with a giggly thrum,
Echoing laughter, a fruit-laden drum.

In the shade of old branches, we gather in cheer,
With stories and snacks, we hold each other dear.
A cat in a hat struts with silly flair,
Turning our picnic into a circus affair.

The aroma of fun fills the warm summer air,
While the breeze snickers, pulling our hair.
Fruits of the season, like gems to behold,
With splashes of humor in stories retold.

So let the sun shine, let the giggles resound,
In this haven of laughter, delight knows no bound.
We sway in the rhythm of nature's own beat,
As delectable moments make life feel complete.

A Symphony of Warmth

In a garden where giggles bloom,
Fruits dance to a jolly tune.
Bouncing like jesters, round and ripe,
They whisper secrets, oh what a type!

With each bite, a chuckle bursts,
Juices flow, oh how it thirsts!
The laughter of flavors, bright and merry,
A fiesta of joy, not one can be dreary!

So gather your friends for a fruity spree,
Savor the jokes that hang from the tree.
Play hide and seek among the vines,
In this fruity realm, all the sun shines!

We twirl and spin, oh what a treat,
Comedic moments, oh so sweet.
In this funny garden where giggles stand,
Laughter ripens, so heartily planned!

The Ritual of Autumn's Bounty

Leaves are swirling, a jolly parade,
Fruits plump and cheerful, never to fade.
There's a ritual dance, with a wink and a grin,
As baskets overflow with a whimsical spin.

Harvesting joy with a clumsy delight,
Hands sticky with goodness, oh what a sight.
Each fruit a joker, each smile a treat,
A laughter-filled day, oh isn't it neat?

Neighbors chuckle, their faces aglow,
As they barter their wares with a friendly row.
"Take my apples!" "Here, have a pear!"
Oh, what a sight, summer's end we'll share!

Under the harvest moon, we'll feast and play,
In this funny gathering, joy leads the way.
With hiccups of laughter and munches galore,
The season wraps us in joy evermore!

Gentle Drops of Stardust

Morning dew glistens, mirth to bestow,
On leaves that giggle, putting on a show.
Dancing sunbeams make shadows collide,
Here in the orchard, silliness hides.

Fruit stars twinkle, their laughter we hear,
As bumblebees buzz with humor sincere.
Each drip of nectar, a punchline well told,
Nature's comedy that never grows old.

With friends by my side, we wander and roam,
In this charming orchard, we've made our home.
Each bite is a giggle that tickles the air,
Sprinkling stardust, with giggles to share.

As twilight arrives, the moon joins the fun,
Lighting our path as we run and we run.
With laughter and joy, we dance in delight,
In this cosmic playground, all feels so right!

Fragrant Pathways Beneath the Trees

In a grove where aromas tickle the nose,
Footsteps echo, as adventure grows.
Beneath the branches, the fruits play tricks,
Each and every bite gives our taste buds kicks.

A scent of mischief wafts in the air,
As we navigate pathways with laughter to spare.
The trees chuckle softly, their whispers so clear,
"Join the feast here, with good cheer, my dear!"

We hop and skip, with baskets in hand,
Finding the juiciest gems in the land.
With giggles and grins, it's a comical spree,
This fragrant journey is as fun as can be!

As dusk approaches, and stars start to peek,
We share our tales, laughter loud with a cheek.
In the fragrant paths where the fruits take the lead,
We find joy in abundance, oh yes, indeed!

A Symphony of Flavors

In orchards bright, the laughter flows,
With every bite, the humor grows.
A pear's soft giggle, oh what a sound,
Each juicy morsel, joy unbound.

Beneath the tree, a dance begins,
With wobbly steps and giddy grins.
Pears in a waltz, they shimmy and sway,
As critters gather, they come out to play.

In kitchen chaos, a recipe's fun,
Spilling juice, oh what a run!
A pear pie that failed, a comical sight,
With crust on the ceiling, oh what a fright!

So raise a glass to each flavor blend,
For laughs and fruits will never end.
With every slice of nature's cheer,
Life's funny moments, we hold dear.

Honeyed Moments

Lemon zest and pear delight,
Bouncing jokes, oh what a sight.
Sipping cider, the giggles flow,
With every gulp, our spirits glow.

Jarred confessions, honeyed dreams,
Sticky fingers, laughter beams.
A pear in hand, a playful tease,
Spilling secrets with such ease.

Behind the counter, mishaps arise,
A pear rolls off; oh, what a surprise!
With butterfingers, we're dancing around,
As the fruit goes flying and hits the ground!

So let's raise our forks, and toast to these,
A bowl of laughter, like summer breeze.
With every moment, a taste of glee,
In honeyed memories, we're always free.

Juicy Secrets of the Grove

In shady groves where mischief starts,
Pears whisper secrets, oh how it sparks.
Funny tales of fruit so bold,
With trickster roots, their stories told.

Dancing ants on a picnic spread,
Sipping nectar, so much said.
Laughter bubbles among the vines,
Juicy whispers from pear to pines.

A pear's grand plot to steal the show,
With giggles ripe, and laughter flow.
Mixing flavors in a punch bowl,
The fun erupts, it's good for the soul!

So savor each laugh, let freshness roam,
In pear-filled fun, we find our home.
For hidden secrets, both bright and clear,
Bring joy and laughter, year after year.

Sun-Kissed Memories

Under the sun, a picnic's pride,
Pears unwrapped, joy amplified.
Laughter's echoed in the air,
As fruity puns dance everywhere.

With berry hats, and jokes to spare,
A pear parade, with zest to share.
Squirrels chuckling, join the feast,
With fruity chaos, never ceased.

When summer's blush brings carefree glee,
Pears frolic under the willow tree.
A fruit fight breaks, what a sight to see,
With sticky friendships, wild and free!

So gather close, let's toast our cheer,
To pear-filled days, with friends so dear.
In sun-kissed memories, let laughter steer,
Chasing the joy from year to year.

Underneath the Canopy's Glow

In the park where laughter sways,
Beneath the branches, sunlit haze,
The squirrels dance with acorn dreams,
While ducks plot their silly schemes.

A picnic blanket, spread just right,
I drop my sandwich, what a sight!
Ants hold a feast, I'm in their way,
They march as if it's a grand parade!

With lemonade spilling on my shoes,
The bees buzz loudly, breaking news,
A grasshopper joins in the fun,
He hops and hops, we all just run!

The sun dips low, a silly end,
As shadows stretch, the colors blend,
We're off to chase the firefly glow,
Who knew nature had such a show?

Embracing Nature's Gentle Gifts

Berries lying under green trees,
They laugh and giggle in the breeze,
A rabbit hops, then stops to stare,
At the pie crust set out with care.

A wind that whispers silly tales,
Of giggly frogs and minor fails,
The garden gnomes are in a race,
One trips and lands in dirt's embrace!

With flowers winking in the sun,
A bumblebee says 'Join the fun!'
It buzzes round my nose with glee,
I swat but only end up free!

In nature's arms, we spin around,
Under the sky's funny clown mound,
We'll dance until the day is through,
With every laugh, our spirits grew!

Melting into the Harvest Moon

Under the harvest moon's soft glow,
The pumpkins giggle, putting on a show,
A patch of squash starts to collaborate,
With cornstalks swaying, they celebrate!

The cider spills, oh what a splash,
A rolling apple goes by in a flash,
The leaves join in, a rustling cheer,
As critters scamper, spreading good cheer!

A raccoon wears a tiny hat,
He tries to juggle—oh, imagine that!
With pies on windowsills, we'll all convene,
To munch on goodies fit for a queen!

As twilight dims the bright parade,
We toast with mugs, no plans mislaid,
The harvest moon, a grand finale,
Our laughter echoing down the alley!

Curled in the Warmth of Familiarity

On a couch with friends, we share a snack,
A mountain of chips, no turning back,
With dip galore, a splattered scene,
Who knew friendship could be so keen?

Tales of rich pranks and fumbled trends,
We giggle and snort, this glee never ends,
A cat jumps in, claiming our space,
As laughter erupts, we can't keep pace!

The ice cream melts, a sticky mess,
Popsicle sticks stick on my dress,
Blame it on summer, oh the delight,
In a whirl of fun, we revel all night!

As stars peek through, our hearts are full,
In moments like this, time takes a pull,
Curling closer, wrapped in this glow,
Our silly chaos is all we know!

Tender Temptations

In a garden where giggles bloom,
Pears dance lightly, avoiding the broom.
They tickle the wind, roll over the ground,
Creating chaos, such joy can be found.

A silly pear juggles, its friends stand around,
With each wobbly toss, they all hit the ground.
Laughter erupts as they tumble and cheer,
Who knew fruit could cause such a raucous atmosphere?

Beneath the bright sun, they plan their next game,
A pear in a hat claims, "We'll rise to fame!"
They race through the vines, with giggles and glee,
Taking bets on who rolls faster, you see?

In this orchard of fun, life's juicy and bright,
With pears as our hosts, we revel in delight.
So raise up your glass, let the laughter invade,
For moments like these are forever displayed.

Serene Fruits of Nature

In a leafy domain where the chuckles abound,
Comical pears wear their laughter like crowns.
They swing from the branches with juicy delight,
Squeezing the giggles from morning to night.

Bouncing with glee, a pear takes a dive,
While its pals gather 'round, full of jive.
They splash in a puddle, all covered in green,
What a sight to behold, all so comically keen!

Off to the picnic, they bring all their flair,
A sandwich, a pie, and a pear in despair.
For though it was ripe, it was squished in the sack,
Yet laughter, sweet laughter, never will lack.

In nature's embrace where humor runs free,
These pears make a ruckus, a wild jubilee.
So join in their antics, let your joy unfurl,
For life's little oddities add zest to the whirl.

Blossom and Bounty

In the orchard of joys, where hilarity reigns,
Pears tell their tales in delightfully funny chains.
With cheeky little grins and their bouncy small frame,
Each burst of laughter builds up to their fame.

Blossoms wave hello to the jovial crew,
As pears spin in circles, their friends bid adieu.
They frolic through fields, on a joyful spree,
Each roll in the grass adds more laughter, you see!

Gathering for storytime under the sun,
A pear tells a tale, and the audience's fun.
With each twist and turn, they all gasp and cheer,
"Life's juicier moments just need a good peer!"

So grab a ripe pear and join in the play,
In this silly orchard where laughter holds sway.
With blossoms around and good company near,
Each moment of joy is a moment so dear.

Glistening at Dusk

As evening descends, a soft giggle is heard,
Pears twirling in dusk light, quite comical, absurd.
They gather together for a grand little show,
With twinkling lights on and giggles in tow.

Wobbling around, they're a sight to behold,
In the warm twilight, their laughter is gold.
A pear in a tutu, dancing by chance,
Makes quite the spectacle, sparking the dance!

They play hide and seek beneath twinkling stars,
Hiding behind blossoms, pretending to spar.
Each time they get found, the sound of their glee,
Echoes through twilight, a joyous decree.

So as dusk settles soft on this playful parade,
Pears keep on laughing, their charm won't ever fade.
For in every giggle lies a memory of cheer,
Glistening at dusk, showcasing joy so near.

www.ingramcontent.com/pod-product-compliance
Lightning Source LLC
Chambersburg PA
CBHW070312120526
44590CB00017B/2644